Credit Repair Hacks 101

Simple Guide on Building Good Credit & Maintaining Financial Wellness

First Edition

Brandon Bell
CEO/Owner Bellman & Associates Inc.
Shaw University Graduate 16'
Regent University School of Law 18'

Strategies on Raising Your Score from 500 to 800 Quickly

Name: Bell, Brandon., 1990-
Title: **Credit Repair Hacks 101: Simple Guide on Building Good Credit & Maintaining Financial Wellness.**
Description: First Edition. | Durham, NC: Bellman & Associates Inc. Est. [2018]
Subjects: Credit, Credit Repair, Business—United States

Bellman & Associates Inc.
Raleigh, NC 27610
brandonbellenterprise@gmail.com
ISBN: 9798670342308

Dedication

I dedicate this book to my MOM, close family and friends. To Alnita Williams, who continues to push me into greater and higher depths. To Akameen Daughtridge, who continues to challenge me to step out of fear and step into faith. To Dr. Janice Thomas, who continues to encourage me to go above and beyond and reach my highest potential.

Terms/ Use of Book

This book was designed to provide educational information regarding credit repair. The publisher has strived to be as accurate and complete as possible in the creation of this report, notwithstanding the fact that he does not warrant or represent at any time that the contents within are accurate due to the rapidly changing nature of the Internet. While all attempts have been made to verify information provided in this publication, the Publisher assumes no responsibility for errors, omissions, or contrary interpretation of the subject matter herein.

Readers are cautioned to reply on their own judgment about their individual circumstances to act accordingly. This book is not intended for use as a source of legal, business, accounting or financial advice. All readers are advised to seek services of competent professionals in legal, business, accounting, and finance field.

This book is also designed to give you strategies and techniques to help you improve your credit score. If after you read this book and you will like additional help with your credit, you can call Bellman & Associates Inc., to pull your credit report and send you a copy. You can contact our office at 919-891-4735 or send us an email at brandonbellenterprise@gmail.com and we will send you the form. Remember, Bellman & Associates Inc., is not a credit repair agency and we do not assume the responsibility as one. We will only pull credit reports and tell you where you need improvement at.

Introduction

First, I want to say, I am so proud of you for taking the first step in taking the initiative to improve your credit and becoming financially literate. I know that this can be one of the biggest stressors in your life, but I want to assure you that you will be able to raise your score and live the life you want to live. You will be able to get the car of your dreams, the house of your dreams, and be able to build an empire and leave a legacy for your children and generations to come.

So, lets go and fix your credit … you ready? Let's go.

One thing about the United States is that we are in debt. It's not just the government, it's not just the businesses, but it's the Americans, the individuals. The problem isn't the fact that we are not able to fix it, it's the mentality that we have about financial success and that fact that we are not educated enough about credit and financial wellness. We believe that it takes years and even decades for us to fix our credit and to become financially free. How is this? Many times, we are not taught at a young age on the advantages and disadvantages of credit and how it can affect us when we get older.

But think about this, according to recent studies and

research from the 2019 Credit Risk Management, 90% of Americans have at least one credit card. Well that's good right? In the instance that one is not educated on how it can affect them in the long run, they will use that card a lot and carry an average balance of more than $7,000. The high number comes from missed payments, late fees, and interests. Many families have an average of $1,000 of interest a year on credit cards.

What could you have done with that $1,000? Invested? Maybe put in a high interest yielding savings account? Put it up for your children's education fund?

When you think about money that you could have saved, it gives you an initial thought of creating other innovative ways to start investing money; ways to save money, and investing in educating yourself on how to improve your credit scores. With this book, it will give you the strategies and techniques you need to help improve your score and give you innovative ways to build credit and savings.

The truth is that you can get out of debt and repair your credit nearly to what it was before you had credit problems. It takes some time and a little work on your part, but it IS possible. Loan approvals and such depend on your credit score.

That number is what determines if you can get credit, what your interest rate will be, and how much money potential lenders will give you. A good median score is 750, but the higher your score is, the more financially sound you are. While it's always a good idea to try and stay away from credit, not everyone has a hundred thousand dollars lying around to buy a home or twenty thousand to buy a car.

Heck, for some people, scraping together three thousand dollars for a good used car is even difficult. That is where credit would come in. So, we can buy that which we cannot afford. That way, we are able to enjoy the luxuries of having something that technically isn't ours just yet. Sounds a little harsh, but that is the true reality of what we see and face in America as individuals. Where the trouble comes in is when people begin to buy everyday items such as groceries and clothing on credit cards. Then those bills begin to get bigger and bigger until pretty soon, they're paying the minimum amount due which will take forever to pay off.

Truth is, the reason why lower-class individuals are so quick to get credit cards is so they can temporarily survive, even if they know the long-term consequences that could come from using the cards. But the truth of the matter is, it is survival of the fittest. Plus, a lot of people just continue charging things even when they have a large balance on their account. This book is designed to help you overcome these difficult situations as well as give you realistic tips and strategies on building your credit.

Your credit score defines who you are to businesses and you want it to be as high as it can be. It doesn't matter how bad your credit is now. There are ways that you can raise your credit score no matter how low it is. Don't get worried about what the number says now. Everyone has to crawl before they walk, so even a 20-point increase is better than no increase at all. Keep at it and continue to soar past what number you see. Imagine where you want to be. Write down a number and work your way to that number. Wait, I heard what you just said.

"How am I going to see myself at a 720 and right now I am at a 580. That's not realistic!"

Well it's not about where you are now. It's about where you are going and where you want to be. See yourself at a 720 and watch your score go up. Faith without works is dead, so let's get to work.

Realistic Story, I was in college and I had the opportunity to get a credit card with a $1,000 credit limit. As a young man in college, uneducated about credit, I was like "yeah," I'm about to go and buy some new clothes, shoes, and ended up spending $700+ dollars in one day. In about three months, the bill was over my credit limit. Literally, it took me about two years to pay off the balance, but what you don't understand is that it took me two years to pay off one day of spending. So, I am here to help you pay off your balance faster than me, as well as, give you information on credit hacks and how to properly use credit cards.

Chapter One

Credit Scores v. Credit Report(s)

This chapter is designed to educate you on your credit score, your credit report, and how credit reporting works. This is very important on how to move forward with understanding your credit and how you can improve it.

What is your Credit Score?

I know you are saying, "I know what my credit score is," but just looking at your score is not what your score is. There are so many components to this. But in academic terms, your credit score is actually the numeric summary or "grade" for all the information that is in your credit report. Sounds about right? Yes, because that's exactly what it is.

Your credit score and underlying history are some of the most vital parts of your financial life. Your credit score follows you forever and it will play a huge role in many major financial situations throughout your life. Many people think that a credit score only really matters when it comes to being approved for a loan or credit card, but it goes far beyond that.

Credit scores range from 300 to 850 (the higher the better) and aren't automatically included with your credit report, but you can order them separately. Your credit report directly influences your credit score with positive reporting from your creditors helping your score and negative information hurting your score. You can have a great score with factors that have hurt your score and you can have a poor score with factors that have a low impact on your score, that could essentially help your score in the short term.

What is your Credit Report?

The very first step you need to take when trying to raise your credit score is to find out what your score is and what it means. Legislation called the FACT Act was passed that allows all Americans to get one free copy of their credit report every year.

This report lists all of your debts you've had and your payment history on those debts. It will tell you where you owe money, how much you owe, and how you pay (on time, 30 days late, etc.). All of that information is compiled together and then analyzed. After the analysis, a number is assigned to you as to what your credit fitness level is.

Potential creditors then look at your credit score and decide if you are going to be able to pay back the amount of money you are requesting to borrow.

That is actually the shorter version of what your credit report is. There are actually much more components in your report that will help determine your score. Your Credit Report and your Credit Score go hand in hand in trying to establish financial wellness.

The biggest thing is understanding your score, understanding how to read your score, and how to raise that score so that you are able to get the things you need. Remember that – the things you NEED, not the things you WANT!

You may have an idea about what your credit report contains but you'd be surprised to find that there can be errors on your report. This is sometimes common for people that never look at their credit report and don't pay attention to certain things on their report.

That is why it is important for you to check your credit report and for you to make sure that there are no errors on it. It's okay, don't be scared to check your credit. Because scared credit can't get no credit.

Chapter Two

"What is FICO"

Some of you may recall that back in the 1960's, there was a company called Fair Isaac that devised a unique system to determine the credit worthiness of people who applied for loans. Through a complicated mathematical computation (too complicated for me to try to explain it to you) , they were able to study a person's credit history and assign them a number that would represent how likely it was that they would be able to repay a loan they were applying for. It pretty much sounds like what we have today, but it was more complicated due to the technological disadvantages that they didn't have back then. Information is always changing and forever evolving, so now this process is much more up-to-date.

Fair Isaac sparked a revolution by pioneering credit risk scoring for the financial services industry. This new approach to lending enabled financial institutions to improve their business performance and expand consumers' access to credit.

Today Fair Isaac's FICO score is widely recognized as the industry standard for lenders. The FICO score condenses a borrower's credit history into a single number based on past credit history. Fair, Isaac & Co. and the credit bureaus do not reveal how these scores are computed.

The Federal Trade Commission has ruled this to be acceptable. The real truth is that even if we did know, we probably couldn't calculate it ourselves anyway. Unless, of course, you happen to be a mathematical genius because clearly, I am not when it comes down to this right here. Oh, come on, laugh, its just a joke. No, but seriously, I cant help you in that area.

Truth is that credit scores are calculated by using scoring models and mathematical tables that assign points for different pieces of information which best predict future credit performance. Developing these models involves studying how thousands, even millions, of people have used credit. Score-model developers find predictive factors in the data that have proven to indicate future credit performance. Models can be developed from different sources of data.

Credit-bureau models are developed from information in consumer credit-bureau reports. Credit scores analyze a borrower's credit history considering numerous factors such as:

Late payments, average length of credit, debt to income ratio, and negative credit information such as, bankruptcies, charge-offs, collections etc. Collections and charge-offs are the most common in America because truth is, many Americans cannot afford to pay certain bills and it goes into collections by a collection agency, which then takes about seven years to fall off if there is no payment made.

Fair Isaac has become so important in the financial industry that their word on your credit has become basically the final word. Why would banks and creditors place so much credibility into one company? The answer is simply because of their proven track record.

The FICO score has proven to be not only an accurate and amazingly consistent way of showing a person's credit reliability, but it has also saved companies millions of dollars in credit write-offs due to bad lending decisions. A study of loans that were granted and/or denied simply due to the FICO scores shows that Fair Isaac has been right over 80 percent of the time. Of course, that required some chance taking on the part of many creditors, but they were willing to take the risk. After all, this was a ground-breaking thing determining credit worthiness through a simple three-digit number.

Bring it to the twenty-first century and you will find that FICO has become the definitive when it comes to financial and credit matters. They have proven their reliability and their worthiness just through trial and error. Unfortunately, the problem is that finding your FICO score isn't as easy as you think.

The truth is that it's not even shown on your credit report like you would think. In fact, for years and years, your credit score was a securely kept secret number that was elusive to the average person. So how can you find out your credit score? I often wondered the same thing and thought that Experian, Equifax, and TransUnion was the only three areas in which I was able to get my score. But after countless hours of extensive research and educating myself on credit and how to build, I finally was able to figure it out.

The first thing you should do is order copies of all three of your credit histories from the major reporting bureaus Equifax, Experian, and TransUnion. The next section is geared towards where you can get your reports as well as gives you the websites and information on how you can get your free reports, but watch out, there are certain stipulations that could trick you. But that is why I am here to give you the hacks.

Chapter Three

"How to Obtain Your Credit Reports"

You would think that finding out what your credit score is would be easy. In a way it is, but only because I've done my research and you won't have to spend time surfing websites looking for the ever elusive credit number. It would seem logical to have your credit score appear right on your credit report, but that's just not the way it is.

At one time, your credit score was a big secret known only to financial companies and banks. With the FACT Act, legislators decided that it was important for individuals to know not only what their personal credit scores are but how they are calculated and how to improve them.

The main company who calculates your credit score is the Field, Isaac Company commonly known as FICO. They invented the concept of the FICO scores so they are the ones who are known as experts in the industry.

Before we go into finding your score, let's look at a few facts about the FICO score. This particular score as discussed earlier is your "credit rating." Scores can range from a low of 300 to a high of 850. Which do you think is better? You got it! I would say anything in the 700s is a plus for me, but of course, we all have our own expectations.

FICO scores are calculated based on your rating in five general categories:

[1] Payment history - 35%

[2] Amounts owed - 30%

[3] Length of credit history - 15%

[4} New credit - 10%

[5] Types of credit used - 10%

In many lending situations, the lender bases its decision almost solely on your credit score. Consider your credit score the overall GPA of your borrowing history. Now, here's the bad news. If you want to know your actual credit score, you will usually have to purchase it.

Credit reports and credit scores can cost money, especially if you don't know where to go or how to obtain them. If you are ordering them frequently throughout the credit repair process, you can easily spend over a hundred dollars. Good thing there are places that you can get your credit report and credit score for free or inexpensively.

AnnualCreditReport.com This is a website through which you can order the free credit reports that you're entitled to by federal law. To make sure you're taking advantage of this right, you must order through AnnualCreditReport.com.

FreeCreditScore.com Your credit score through FreeCreditScore.com can be acquired for free which is based on your Experian credit report. But to do so you must be enrolled in a trial subscription to a credit monitoring service. Failing to cancel within seven days will result in a monthly credit card charge. REMEMBER TO CANCEL YOUR SUBSCRIPTION!!

MyFICO.com The only place you can get a free FICO score, the score most commonly used by lenders, is through myFICO.com. There's a catch, though. To get your free FICO score, you must sign up for a trial subscription to Score Watch, a credit score monitoring service. If you don't cancel – you guessed it – your credit card will be charged.

CreditKarma.com Here, you can get a free credit score without having to enter any credit card number. You don't have to enroll in a trial subscription, and you don't have to cancel anything to avoid being charged. The score is your TransUnion credit score which is based on data from that credit report. An advantage this site offers is you can order an updated credit score through Credit Karma as often as you'd like, for free.

Quizzle.com Quizzle gives you access to both your credit report and credit score – for free. There's no credit card required, and you don't have to cancel a subscription to anything. They don't even need your social security number. Both the credit report and score are based on your data at Experian. You can get a free credit score and report from Quizzle twice a year.

Chapter 4

"Understanding Your Credit Report"

When you receive each report, go over every single line of information and check for accuracy. Any information that is not correct should be reported back to the credit bureau using the online or printed forms provided. The bureaus are required to investigate all reported inaccuracies and if the creditor does not cooperate, the information may be dropped from your report. Unfortunately, credit reports aren't the most intuitive documents. When you're checking your credit report for the first time, you may be confused about the layout and the information that's being reported.

Some credit reports are easier to understand than others. The simplest ones use different fonts and colors to separate the sections. Those that are harder to understand usually use a typewriter-looking font, include codes, and use little spacing. Most credit reports sections are laid out in the same order.

Personal information lists your name, name variations (e.g. if you've been married or sometimes use a middle initial), current and previous addresses, phone number, date of birth, entire or last four digits of your social security number, and employer.

The summary section varies by credit report but typically gives a highlight of the negative information on your credit report, like the number of negative accounts and the total amount past due. The summary section may also provide information about your total credit age and sum amount of credit card and loan balances.

The largest section of your credit report lists details about all your credit accounts individually. For each credit card, loan, collection account, etc. the same basic information is reported: [1] Information about the creditor, [2] Status of the account, e.g. whether you're current or past due, [3] Date the account was opened, [4] Last time the account was updated, [5] Type of account, e.g. installment, revolving, collection, etc. [6] Credit limit or original loan amount [7] High balance (this is the highest balance charged on the account), [8] Current balance [9] Account history for the past seven years, and [10] Your personal statement for the account Public records include things like bankruptcy, repossession, foreclosure, and judgments that are on file with a court system.

Inquiries are added to your credit report whenever a business requests to see your credit report. Some inquiries are added because of your applications for credit. These "hard" inquiries are on all your credit reports and are used to calculate your credit scores. Other inquiries are done by you, employers, existing creditors, and businesses that want to pre-approve you. These "soft" inquiries only show up on your credit report and are not used to calculate your score.

Reading about what's in your credit report doesn't fully help you understand your credit report. Fortunately, there are a few tutorials out there provided by the same people who put your credit report together.

How to Read Your Report

Analyze every bit of information listed on the credit report, including your name, address, Social Security number, and all account information. Any information that is inaccurate should be jotted down for later reference. Each credit bureau will have an online or printed form where you can list incorrect information. All consumer requests must be investigated by the credit bureau once they have been received.

Investigations can change the status of the report information if found to be false. In some cases, the creditor will not comply with the request for information and subsequently the incorrect data will be dropped from the report. By updating and correcting information, your report will reflect a more accurate picture of your financial health and be an asset for you when applying for new credit, looking for a new job, renting a home, and even getting insurance quotes.

Negative Factors that Hurt Your Score

Recent delinquencies Recent delinquencies, especially 90+ day payments, can adversely affect your score. Payment history is 35% of your credit score, so late payments can take their toll on your credit score. Charge-offs, debt collections, bankruptcies, repossession, foreclosure, lawsuit judgments, and tax liens also fall under the payment history portion of your credit score. Any unpaid bill Any unpaid bill can become a serious delinquency, even if it's not a credit card or loan.

Many businesses now send even the smallest debts to a collection agency if that debt goes unpaid. Since collection agencies almost always add debts to your credit report, a $5.00 library fine or a $35 phone bill can end up on your credit report and hurt your scores. Maxed-out credit card balances

The second-most important part of your credit score includes your credit card and balances. The closer your credit card balances are to your credit limit, the worse it is for your credit score. The same thing goes for any loan balances. If you have loan balances that are over or close to the loan amount, your credit score will be hurt. Many experts recommend using no more than 30% of your allotted credit extension to improve and maintain your credit score.

Closed accounts that still have balances It's common for people to close their credit cards simply because they're upset with the credit card company or because they don't want the temptation of the credit card anymore. Unfortunately, this doesn't hurt the credit card company, but it does hurt your credit score. Once your credit card is closed, your credit limit is usually reported as $0. If your credit card has a balance, it looks like you've maxed-out when all you've really done is closed the account. Too many recent credit applications Inquiries count for 10% of your credit score.

Your score takes a hit whenever you put in several credit card or loan applications. Each time you apply for credit, an inquiry is placed on your credit report. Ten percent doesn't sound like much, but that means too many inquiries can cost you 65 points on a 650 credit score. Newly opened credit accounts Fifteen percent (15%) of your credit score is based your credit age. This includes the amount of time since you opened your first account and the average age of all your credit accounts. Opening a new account lowers your average credit age and can hurt your credit score.

How Long Does Bad Credit Stay on Your Record

You may have had a few bad months or even a few bad years when debt got out of hand and financial obligations became uncontrollable. After missing three or four payments on your credit card accounts or other bills, your credit report will begin to reflect negative payment information and your credit score will begin its decent. As a general rule, 7 years is the length of time a credit report will show an accurate negative mark but it is more complex than that.

Hint Hint *Here are the exceptions to the 7-year rule of credit reports*:

1.   Bankruptcy If you have filed for bankruptcy, the information will be reported on your credit history for the following 10 years.

2.   Tax Liens If you had a lien filed against you for taxes owed to the government, the information will remain on your credit history report for 7 years from the date you paid the debt.

Loan Default- If you default on a loan with the U.S. government or a guaranteed student loan the information can be reported for 7 years after the guarantor takes action. Lawsuits Judgments against you in a lawsuit can be reported to your credit history for seven years or for the period specified in the statute of limitations, whichever is longer. Make sure to check with your loan companies to be sure that you are in good standing

Chapter 5

"Repairing Your Credit Score"

Don't get weary in this part of the process. In order to get the score, you desire you must be willing to face the reality and stay focused. We are all humans and we all make mistakes in life. Some of us make mistakes far greater than missing a bill or allowing an account to go to collections, so stay calm and smile, better days are ahead.

The key to this though is to recognize that your spending habits are out of control, your credit has been damaged, and then vow to never get yourself back in the same situation after you have gotten your credit repaired.

Order your credit reports. Then go over those credit reports carefully. I explained to you earlier how to read your score. It will be a breeze. If you don't understand it the first time, go back and try again. This time , slow down and you will be just fine.

Check to see that there are no errors such as a bill you've paid but that is still being shown as owed. People at credit bureaus are human too and make mistakes just like you! If you don't call attention to these mistakes, no one else will. The next part involves pulling out those accounts that are delinquent and making a re-payment plan. Unless you are declaring bankruptcy, you'll still need to pay your debts and doing so can go a long way towards improving your credit history. Creditors will see that you are doing the best you can to get back on your feet and this improves your credibility

Most creditors, however, look for a pattern of payment rather than focusing on one-time or rare occurrences. That's why consistent on-time bill payments will improve those blemishes. As soon as you have paid off your creditors, then you can start all over again.

Experts say the average time required to rebuild one's credit to the point at which you can be accepted for a major credit card or small loan is approximately two years. Here are some other things to consider when trying to repair your score

1. **Pay down your credit cards!!** Paying off your installment loans (mortgage, auto, student, etc.) can help your score, but typically not as dramatically as paying down -- or paying off -- revolving accounts like credit cards. Getting your balances below 30% of the credit

limit on each card can really help. While most debt gurus recommend paying off the highest-rate card first, a better strategy here is to pay down the cards that are closest to their limits.

2. **Use your cards lightly!!** Racking up big balances can hurt your score, regardless of whether you pay your bill in full each month. What's typically reported to the credit bureaus, and thus calculated into your score, is the balance reported on your last statement. That doesn't mean paying off your balances each month isn't financially smart -- it is -- just that the credit score doesn't care. You typically can increase your score by limiting your charges to 30% or less of a card's limit. If you're having trouble keeping track, consider using a check register to track your spending, logging into your account frequently at the issuer's Web site, or using personal finance software like Microsoft Money or Quicken, which can download your transactions and balances automatically.

3. **Check your limits!!** Your score might be artificially depressed if your lender is showing a lower limit than you've actually got. Most credit-card issuers will quickly update this information if you ask. If your issuer makes it

a policy not to report consumers' limits, however -- as is the usual case with American Express cards and those issued by Capital One -- the bureaus typically use your highest balance as a proxy for your credit limit. You may see the problem here: If you consistently charge the same amount each month -- say $2,000 to $2,500 -- it may look to the credit scoring formula like you're regularly maxing out that card. You could go on a wild spending spree to raise the limit, but a more sober solution would simply be to pay your balance down or off before your statement period closes. It won't raise your reported limit, but it will widen the gap between that limit and your closing balance, which should boost your score.

4. **Get some goodwill.** If you've been a good customer, a lender might agree to simply erase that one late payment from your credit history. You usually have to make the request in writing, and your chances for a "goodwill adjustment" improve the better your record with the company (and the better your credit in general). But it can't hurt to ask. A longer-term solution for more-troubled accounts is to ask that they be "re-aged." If the account is still open, the lender might erase previous delinquencies if you make a series of 12 or so on-time

payments. When trying to improve your credit score or credit history, avoid any of the following:

5. **Asking a creditor to lower your credit limits**. This will reduce that all important gap between your balances and your available credit, which could hurt your score. If a lender asks you to close an account or get a limit lowered as a condition for getting a loan, you might have to do it -- but don't do so without being asked.

6. **Avoid making a late payment.** The irony here is that a late or missed payment will hurt a good score more than a bad one, dropping a 700-plus score by 100 points or more. If you've already got a string of negative items on your credit report, one more won't have a big impact, but it's still something you want to avoid if you're trying to improve your score.

7. **Consolidating your accounts.** Applying for a new account can ding your score. So, too, can transferring balances from a high-limit card to a lower limit one, or concentrating all or most of your credit-card balances onto a single card. In general, it's better to have smaller balances on a few cards than a big balance on one.

Laws to Know During Credit Repair and Beyond

Did you know there are laws that protect your rights before, during, and even after credit repair? Repairing your credit requires you to work with giant companies who have a lot more money than you. These companies would have complete power over the credit repair process, if the government hadn't put a few rules in place to keep these companies in check. The law isn't perfect and some companies find loopholes, but knowing the law can help you get results.

Fair Credit Reporting Act The FCRA is a law that generally dictates what can and can't appear on your credit report. The FCRA says that inaccurate, incomplete, unverifiable, or outdated information can't be listed on your credit report. You have the right to dispute credit report errors either with the credit bureau or the company that listed the information on your credit report. It was an amendment to the FCRA in 2003 that entitles you to your annual credit reports through the federally mandated AnnualCreditReport.com.

Fair Credit Billing Act

The FCBA was created to help consumers correct billing errors from credit card companies. Billing errors include unauthorized charges to your credit card, unposted payments, or charges for merchandise that weren't received as promised. You have 60 days from the date of the billing error to make a dispute directly to the credit card company and the credit card company must investigate the dispute. In the meantime, you don't have to pay for the disputed charges and you can't receive any penalty when you don't pay.

Fair Debt Collection Practices Act The FDCPA is a law that dictates what debt collectors can and cannot do when they're collecting a debt from you. There's a long list of things they can't do. For example, they can't call you before 8 a.m. or after 9 p.m., they can't call if you've already told them it's an inconvenient time, and they can't call you at work if you've told them your employer doesn't approve those calls.

They can't tell certain people about your debt, but can get location information from your friends, **neighbors, and relatives.**

Credit Repair Organizations Act

The CROA was created to protect consumers from unscrupulous credit repair agencies. Scams still happen, but many dishonest credit repair companies are caught and charged by the Federal Trade Commission. Credit repair companies can't lie about the services they provide you, they're not supposed to charge you upfront, and they can't ask you to do anything illegal to "repair" your credit. If a credit repair company violates your rights, you can sue them for penalties and damages.

If you have a complaint against any business you've dealt with during the credit repair process, you can report them to the FTC by visiting www.FTCcomplaintassistant.gov or you can call 1-877-FTC-HELP. You can also report these businesses to your state Attorney General or local Better Business Bureau.

Chapter Six

"Establishing Good Credit"

Well I will say this, "If you have never used credit before, I applaud you." You must of used cash all your life to buy the things you wanted. I wish I could have done the same thing. But in reality, having no established credit is just as bad as bad credit because it doesn't signify or give you a reputation how financial responsible you are. Needing credit in the future are very real. Someday you might want to buy a house. Perhaps you'll want to buy a new car, unless of course you are a millionaire of course.

But reality is the chances are pretty good that you won't have the cash outright to buy these high-ticket items which mean you'll need credit. Plus, it's always good to have a little credit since many utility companies will look at your credit to turn on your power bill, for example, without a deposit of some type.

When you're starting fresh with no credit history at all, here are a few ways to get a good start on establishing good credit:

[1] Pay your bills on time, especially mortgage or rent payments. Apart from extreme circumstances like

bankruptcy or tax liens, nothing has as big of an impact on your credit history as late payments.

[2] Establish credit early. Having clean, active charge accounts established many years ago will boost your score. If you are averse to credit, on principle, consider setting up automatic monthly payments for, say, utilities and phone on a credit card account and locking the card away where it's not a temptation.

One great way to start establishing credit is to apply for a store credit card (Sears, JC Penney, etc.). Once you get the card, make a few small purchases and pay them off completely. Do this a few times over the course of a year and you'll find yourself with some established credit with an excellent payment history. DO NOT go overboard and buy more than what you can pay for, though. You can also apply for a secured credit card. These cards ask that you place a certain amount of money in your account for which you will receive a charge card. Then you can make purchases up to the amount of money that is in your account. Credit reporting agencies treat these cards just like regular credit cards and look to them as a responsible way for you to establish a good credit history.

So, let's do a quick review on how to establish a good credit history:

1. Apply for a store or gas credit card and make a few charges
2. Ask a loved one to co-sign on a loan
3. Find a respected secured credit card company
4. Open a checking account
5. Don't apply for too many credit cards in too short of a time
6. Check your credit report for any errors
7. Go slowly
8. Don't overspend

Chapter 7

"Removing Negative Information from Your Credit Report"

How Credit Report Disputes Repair Your Credit

Inaccurate negative information hurts your credit score. Checking your credit report is the first step in credit repair. Removing inaccurate information is the next step. What Information Can Be Disputed? Technically, you can dispute anything on your credit report. Federal law requires the credit bureau to remove information that's incomplete, inaccurate, or unverifiable.

[1] Your social security number (sometimes only the last four digits of your SSN appear on your credit report)

[2] Payments reported late that were actually paid on time

[3] Negative information that's passed the credit reporting time limit can be disputed for credit repair

[4] Accounts being reported by two collection agencies at once

[5] Accounts that don't belong to you

[6] Accounts reported as closed that are actually open

[7] Accounts discharged in bankruptcy that are reported delinquent or charged-off How to Make a Credit Report Dispute. If you order your credit report online, you might be inclined to make your credit report dispute online as well. However, this leaves you without the paper trail you'll need if the credit bureau doesn't follow the law. The best way to send your credit report dispute is through the mail.

Write a letter and send it certified mail with return receipt requested. That way you have proof of when the letter was mailed and received. If you have multiple errors for your credit repair list, you should dispute them one at a time. Be careful not to bombard the credit bureau with several dispute letters at once. Instead, send a few, wait, and send a few more. If you send too many disputes at once, the credit bureau might decide your disputes are frivolous and refuse to investigate, which they can do legally.

In your dispute letter make sure you include the reason for the dispute, e.g. the payment reported as late was made on time. It helps to include a copy of the credit report you're disputing with the error highlighted. You should also include copies of any proof you have supporting your claim. Keep the original copy of your proof for your records. Send your dispute to the credit bureau that provided the report you're disputing. Here are the mailing addresses for all three credit bureaus:

Equifax P.O. Box 7404256 Atlanta, GA 30374-0256

Experian Dispute Department P.O. Box 9701 Allen, TX 75013

TransUnion Consumer Solutions P.O. Box 2000 Chester, PA 19022-2000

Once you send your credit report dispute, the credit bureau typically has 30-45 days to do an investigation and send a letter alerting you to the result of the investigation. If your dispute results in a change to your credit report, you'll automatically receive a free copy of your updated credit report. Otherwise, the bureau will send a letter telling you why your dispute was rejected.

Negotiate with Creditors Directly

You have the option to negotiate a settlement with your creditors directly. It is advised that part of your negotiation process involves an agreement by the creditor to stop reporting information to the credit bureau or request that the account be listed as 'paid as agreed' instead of being listed as 'settled' on the credit report. This can help raise your credit score as well as improve your chance of loan approval. There is no guarantee a creditor will agree to the request but it certainly can help you credit wise if they will.

How to Construct a Credit Dispute Letter to Your Creditors After discovering any information you would like to dispute, you'll need to follow through by filling out the appropriate forms provided by the credit bureaus to dispute the information.

Once received by the credit bureaus, each dispute must be investigated and contact will be made with your creditors. If the creditor does not reply to the request for information, the credit bureau may drop the data from your report entirely if the debt is not verified.

If the creditor does respond within the 30 day period, the information will be updated or left as is on your report. The credit bureaus will also send you written correspondence about the results of the investigation. If information is verified by the creditor to the credit bureaus that you do not agree with, you'll need to construct a letter directly to the creditor.

Once the letter has been completed and the documents are attached, send it via Certified/Return Receipt Requested through the US Post Office. This will ensure your dispute letter was delivered and you will have a confirmation of that receipt. Once you receive confirmation, wait three to four weeks before following up on with the creditor by phone if you haven't received any other correspondence.

No Reply on a Dispute

Credit bureaus have the legal obligation to reply to your correspondence within a 30-day time frame. The Fair Credit Reporting Act states that the bureaus must have their investigation completed on your behalf within four weeks. In some cases, things do not go as planned. So, what do you do now? Put on the Pressure. In the event you get no reply, the credit bureau must remove the negative information you disputed effective immediately. This will benefit your credit score and attempts at credit repair.

It is up to you to stay on task and follow up with the credit bureaus. You can send them a letter via Certified/Return Receipt Requested. Keep a copy of the information you are sending. What to Include in the Letter Be sure to create a professional-looking letter that contains your return address. You'll want to inform the credit bureau that they have failed to reply to your initial correspondence and list the date of your first contact.

Restate the FCRA law pertaining to the 30-day rule and put them on notice that they will be in violation of the law if they fail to remove the data. Let them know you have kept detailed notes and copies of all correspondence pertaining to the matter. Keep a professional tone and request that the matter receive immediate attention. Enclose copies of your original correspondence that verifies the 30 days has passed. You should relist the accounts that should be deleted from your credit report due to the lack of response. Be sure to include your name and Social Security number for easy tracking.

Dispute a Consumer Dispute

Many consumers working hard to repair their credit will receive a reply from the agencies that their dispute is being disputed. A reply letter may indicate a frivolous dispute so it will be up to you to take further action.

What To Do Next If you have received a letter stating the credit agency finds your disputes irrelevant or frivolous, you'll need to take further action. Review your original dispute documentation and see what the reason was for your dispute.

Plan to re-file the dispute using other reasoning that is still accurate and sound.

The following lists of inaccurate information may help you find the most relevant for your situation: [1] This is not my account, [2] I didn't pay late during…(list date), [3] Wrong amount listed, [4] Wrong account number listed, [5] Wrong original creditor information listed

[6] Wrong charge-off date listed, [7] Wrong date of last activity noted, [8] Wrong balance listed, [9] Wrong credit limit amount listed, [10] Wrong status listed – there are about 20 possible statuses.

Wrong high credit limit amount listed

What You Should Not Do While it is imperative you dispute erroneous information; you should remember not to hit the credit bureaus with a mountain of disputes all at once. You will only be wasting your time. Follow through with only legitimate disputes and don't attempt to challenge the credit bureaus with every entry in the hopes of having them all removed to boost your credit ratings. Once the credit reporting agencies considers all your disputes irrelevant, they are not legally obligated to change any data, leaving you back at square one.

What is a Charge Off?

A charge off lets lenders know you did not meet the financial obligations with your original creditor and that you still owe a balance on the account. See how much you still owe on the account and how much of it is listed as "past due". Can you pay the account in full now? If so, contact the creditor and find out how to make payment and how long before the information is corrected on your credit report. If you do not have enough money to pay for the account in full, contact the lender or the collection agency handling the account and find out what your options are.

Sometimes they will accept a payment plan toward paying off an account in charge off status; other times they require a lump sum payment. If they do accept payments, ask whether or not they will also update the account on your credit report to show you are making payments. This would show any other companies viewing your credit report that you are making good on this debt – although your credit score itself would not likely improve until the account is paid in full.

Pay for Delete

Consider using a pay for delete. That's when you pay off an account in exchange for having it deleted from your credit report. It isn't always successful as creditors and debt collectors aren't required to remove any accurate information from your credit report. In fact, credit bureaus encourage businesses to leave this information on your credit report.

Ultimately, it's up to the business whether to report an item on your credit report. So that's who you approach with a pay for delete. Which Accounts Are Best for Pay for Delete? Pay for delete strategy won't work with every account. It's a better use of your time to try this negotiation on the entries that are most likely to get a good response.

For example, don't try a pay for delete on accounts that are current, but have past delinquency or accounts that have already been paid off. The accounts that are best for a pay for delete are collections and charge-offs. Negotiating a Pay for Delete Getting a pay for delete is all a matter of negotiation. The agreement you're looking for is this: I'll pay this account if you remove it from my credit report upon receipt of payment. Anytime you make an agreement with an account, you should get that agreement in writing, even if the agreement is made over the phone. Get a signed copy of the agreement before you send payment.

A signed copy of your agreement is the only leverage you have to make sure the creditor or debt collector holds up their end of the deal. You can try to negotiate a pay for delete over the phone, but it's often better to send a letter. In your letter, state that you're willing to pay the debt in exchange for having the account removed from your credit report.

In your letter, it's very important that you don't acknowledge that the debt is yours or make a promise to pay it off other than in exchange for deletion. If you can't afford to pay the entire debt, and the debt is owned by a collection agency, you can try to offer a lower lump-sum payment in exchange for deletion. Debt collectors often buy debts for less than 10% of the face value, so they're like to go for a settlement offer. This is especially true if the account has been through several collection agencies.

Removing Public Records from your Report

You may have to work with an attorney to get public records like foreclosure and repossession removed from your credit report. If you can show that there is something about the entry which is questionable, you may be able to successfully remove it from your credit report. But, the hard part is finding the necessary loopholes. That's where an attorney who's knowledgeable about your state's laws comes in.

Using Debt Validation

The credit reporting agencies are required to remove any collection records which cannot be validated from your reports.

When you send a validation request, you request the debt collector to send proof of the debt you allegedly owe. It is worth noting that some debt collectors don't bother with validation requests and their lack of action will result in the record being removed from your credit report. That does not mean that you no longer have to repay your debt, it only means that it will not be used to calculate your credit score, because the information given to the credit reporting agencies couldn't be validated. While the validation takes place, the collector can't collect on the debt or put it on your credit report until the proof has been sent. Again, send these requests via certified mail with return receipt requested.

Chapter 8 "Review & Conclusion"

Review & Conclusion

Congrats, you have made it to the last part of the book! I am so proud of you for reading thus far. I wanted you to get as much knowledge as you can to be able to get your credit to the point where you wanted it. I want you to know that I have been where you are. I have been in a place where I was at a 580 and I wanted to get my credit in the 700's.

Things can't happen overnight, but the most important part is that things can change with hard work and dedication. I assure you that reading this book, you have now taken the initiative to make the moves.

The very first thing that you must do in order to raise your credit score is to order your free annual credit report and find out what your credit score is. Once you have obtained copies of your credit reports from all three credit reporting agencies: Experian, Equifax, and TransUnion, you must take the time to go over those reports to check for errors and inconsistencies. It is imperative that you correct any mistakes or inconsistencies as soon as possible. This is the most pro-active step you can take for yourself to increase your credit score as mistakes can and do happen.

Look for accounts that were previously delinquent, but which have since been paid off. Find any accounts that were closed or any accounts that aren't yours. Then take steps to correct those errors by contacting the credit bureaus and beginning the process in writing to have these errors removed from the report. This alone can raise your credit score.

Checking your credit report often can also indicate if you have become a victim of identity theft which is something that is happening over and over again with frightening frequency. It affects millions of people and can wreak havoc with your credit rating

That's why it's so important to know about credit and when it should be used as well as when it shouldn't be used. Practice smart credit procedures and don't overextend yourself. You can easily find yourself in trouble before you even know it. Then the time comes to change your spending habits, make smart credit decisions and take steps to raise your credit score. No matter what situation you might find yourself in regarding your credit, you can not only get out of debt, but you can restore your credit and enjoy a high credit score.

It takes time and a little bit of effort, but it certainly can be done. You just need to be diligent about your spending habits and then monitor your credit reports so you know where you stand at any particular time.

Credit is an important part of our society, so cherish your credit history and your credit score. Make it just as important to you as your good name and keep it clean and pristine. It can mean so much to your future and your future is just as important as the present.

You know what they say: The past is the past, the future is the future, but today is a gift – that's why they call it the present!

Good Luck! I'm rooting for you!!

God Bless

About the Author

Brandon Bell, entrepreneur, social justice advocate, and upcoming attorney, holds a Bachelor's degree in Sociology from Shaw University and a Master's Degree in Law from Regent University School of Law. Brandon has a passion for Social Justice and financial wellness. Studying Sociology at Shaw University, Brandon saw the socioeconomic problems that communities face in the world, which led him to pursue a career in the Legal and Financial field. He decided to write this book to help educate disadvantaged individuals of financial wellness and credit repair to help them build generation wealth for families. Helping, inspiring, and motivating people across the world is what he loves to do.

He is the founder and CEO of Bellman & Associates Inc., which is a Christian Based Professional Service Firm that specializes in contracts, financial services, such as financial wellness classes etc., career services, private investigation, etc. Brandon has also authored: *"Life After Conviction: Strategies For Success After A Criminal Conviction,"* which is an inspirational based on the true life story of himself, giving hope to individuals who are trying to overcome the obstacles of their criminal past.

Notes

Please take notes so you can get on track with fixing your credit